CW00418402

THE ULTIMATE GUIDE TO PLANNER & JOURNAL DESIGN

MICHELLE CHITTY

Copyright © 2023 by Michelle Chitty

ISBN: 9798397367844

All rights reserved.

No part of this book may be reproduced in any form or by any electronic, mechanical or photographic means, nor to be stored in storage and retrieval systems, or otherwise copied for public or private use- other than the fair use of brief quotations in a book review, without written permission from the author.

authors
AND CO.

CONTENTS

I dedicate this book to my husband Alan thank you for believing in me, you have always believed in me, even when I didn't believe in myself, you are my support, my strength and my everything.

To my family thank you for your support, without the foundations you created and the years you have been there, I wouldn't be who I am today.

To Beth thank you for helping me piece everything together and find my sparkle again.

To my friends thank you for being there with love, support and encouragement through the good times and the bad.

To all the creatives out there that have a dream. Never doubt yourself or your ideas. You are good enough. Keep being determined, move forward every day and never give up.

Love

Michelle
X

Introduction

So, you're curious to see if you can really make your planner or journal vision a reality. This book will tell you all you need to know.

This process has been put together and refined for over a year. It's something that will keep developing over time, but the core process will never change. I want you to know planner and journal creation is for everyone not just for the few. If you have a vision in your head, you can make this happen, you will need dedication, focus and to understand the key elements of the process, but by the end, you can certainly achieve something beautiful.

A creative process is never really finished, you can spend hours, days, weeks and months going back over old ground refining, tweaking and making sure everything is how it should be. After all there is no point in creating something that is only ok. I know you don't want that, and I don't want that for you. I want you to get to the end of the process and be proud of what you have achieved, holding your planner or journal in your hands for the first time is a truly magical moment. There might be moments that you think 'what am I doing' but I can promise you it will be worth it. If you get stuck remember there is a solution to every problem. There are always ways to work around what seems like barriers.

This book will inspire and excite you with the possibilities. When you are really inspired and excited you have a different energy. This energy always holds space for the best ideas and creates momentum behind those ideas. This ensures if you come up against any obstacles in the process you are more likely to overcome and push through them. You will be determined to find a way because you are emotionally invested.

Before we go into the process ask yourself what has been holding you back so far from creating your planner or journal. Maybe you don't have the time or the technical knowledge, you think you're not good at design or the most common one you just don't know where to start.

You can create time, even if you only have one hour spare in a morning. Using that one hour every day on your project will move you in the right direction no matter how slowly you make progress, you are always going to be closer and in a better place than never starting.

You can always learn the technical design skills and improve. As I always say "there is an inner creative in everyone" so you will have some element of creativity in you, you just need to bring it out.

By adding a planner or journal to your business you get the opportunity to add another income stream. Your planner or journal will work for you in ways you wouldn't have considered before reading this book, which will be covered later. Just know right now that it is about much more than focusing on selling copies for profit.

If by the end of the book you want to learn more about any of the aspects that are talked about here or maybe you learn more visually, then there is an answer. I developed a course so you can learn the process of Planning, Designing and Publishing your planner or journal, in your own time. All that really matters is that you get your idea out into the world for people to use and love.

If you feel that being creative isn't for you I offer a one to one, "done for you" design service. You don't have to design or deal with the technical process, you just have to make a few design choices ensuring that by the end of the process, your design is exactly how you want it. There are so many ways of creating your version of success and adding your dream planner or journal to your business. Or maybe you don't have a business, but this might be the starting point to develop a business around a product. Having worked with a lot of clients there have been different ideas and styles to produce however, I am proud to say no one has ever left my service with something they didn't love and also a perfect product for their business.

You can find more information by visiting my website here –

The Printable Life Website

www.theprintablelife.enlitly.com

Through this book you are going to embark on a creative journey, so you can see what it takes to develop, design and publish your very own branded planner or journal. I am going to share with you what is important, the things you need to consider and the inside look of everything I have developed through my one to one process.

The process is split into three main areas.

1. Planning

In this section you will learn what it takes to plan a good project and everything you need to consider at this stage. It's a stage that gets overlooked but it really shouldn't after all, the famous quote by Benjamin Franklin says, *"If you fail to plan, you are planning to fail"*. The project you will be starting is big so to avoid going off track you will need a structure and an understanding of what your planner or journal can offer to your customers or clients.

In this stage there's little focus on the design itself, it's about the purpose of your idea, the messaging and if your idea is going to fit into your business and work well for you. Consideration of design and physical practicalities will be explored. It is about your customer that will be using it. Usability can make or break a planner or journal. If a planner or journal does not spark a certain amount of joy when it gets used or solves an important problem, it will get left at the back of the cupboard and won't be used.

This stage is such an integral part of the project. Don't miss this out because you are set on your idea all ready. Things can change, develop and become a stronger version of what you thought was already a great idea.

2. Designing

Designing is a subjective process; everyone has their own idea of what is a good or bad design. However, no one is here to judge a good design or a bad design. This process is here to teach you the simplicity of what designing a planner or journal can look like and to take away that overwhelming feeling. You can achieve a crisp and professional finish, but not overcomplicate it after all the great thing about this is that everyone can achieve the end result, they want and overcomplication just doesn't need to be a part of it. Don't forget simplicity is a very beautiful thing, so don't think you have to get extra crazy and throw everything at the page. Sometimes less is almost certainly more. In this section you will learn a simple method of how to put a very professional and clean design together, including your cover and how to format everything.

Don't be scared of this part, design is very personal, and it can feel like you are bearing your soul for the whole world to judge. I can almost guarantee that the majority of your audience will receive your design with excitement and gratitude and the ones that don't, you have to ask yourself were they ever going to be the right client or customer for you anyway. Don't let this be a barrier or to hold yourself back thinking you're not good enough or your design isn't good enough because it absolutely is.

3. Publishing

Publishing is an option for you if you don't want to invest in massive print runs, traditional printing will also be touched upon later. In the publishing process there are a lot of things to consider and a lot of choices to be made. This book will take you through all of them.

I have never wanted printing to be a barrier, there is no secret that printing can be very costly. Finding online publishing has allowed designs to be published in an accessible way. If it hadn't of been so accessible some designs may have never been shown to the world. So don't worry, you won't get to the end of the book and see it say you have to spend thousands on printing.

It might seem a little daunting to you right now, but I want to promise you that once you have moved through each stage it will become clearer. You will feel like this is something you can totally achieve. Try not to think any further ahead into the process at the moment, there is a chance overwhelm could set in and I don't want that for you. Let me reassure you that you're in safe hands, I've been through this process many times.

I want you to really look forward to this journey and the process because it's really transformational on a creative and business level. Read through this book at least once before you go on your own journey, this way you will have a complete understanding before you start and you won't miss anything out.

Feel comfortable using this book in your learning process, don't be precious about the pages, scribble your notes and highlight any parts that you want to remember. I have also included a notes section at the back of the book so you can write key things down as you go, at the end of each section the key learning points will be summarised. Use sticky notes to tab the pages you want to come back to. Use it like the creative process it was intended to be used for and best of all enjoy it.

So.........

It's time to get excited because you are taking your first steps into this journey and actually designing and publishing your very own planner or journal.

Let's get started!

DREAM BIG

This book is about giving you a practical insight into designing and publishing a journal or planner for your business. It will move you from concept all the way through to the end product. I have put everything into a process format however, it may not be a straightforward process and you will have to revisit pages or sections of this book. It might sometimes even feel a little messy but trust me, it will lead you to create something amazing and you will have learnt so much by the end.

Before we get into the practical side of things, I want you to lose yourself for a moment, when we concentrate on the practical things, we minimise our ideas to fit into reality. I don't want you to do that. I want you to imagine your planner or journal exactly how you want it to be. Don't minimise or edit yourself because you think it is beyond the realms of possibility. The practical things can always be worked around later. Take a piece of paper and start writing or sketching everything that you would like to see in your planner or journal. Even if it feels small, insignificant or silly, still write it down or draw it.

There are no limitations in this very moment visualise your planner or journal on the shelves, online or in a store. Where are you going to sell it? What is your planner or journal called? What colours can you see? Think about everything and allow yourself to get lost in a world of creativity and joy. You have an incredible opportunity to create something special. Getting your dream out to the world is only part of the journey it all starts with a spark of inspiration or an idea in your head. That's the beauty of getting creatively inspired, an idea can come from anywhere. Get lost in your world, sit there for a moment and visualise exactly how you want it to be. How do you want someone to feel when they use your creation and what makes it special.

Never start a project by thinking your idea or dream isn't possible, there will always be practical limitations that can be worked around. Start by thinking big. If you put limitations in your mind from the start you don't allow your brain to wander and stumble across what could be the big idea you've been looking for. If you think small you already put everything into a box and your mind doesn't expand, because we stop that from happening. We stifle ourselves in our creativity and what could have been an amazing idea turns into something that is a weaker version. Your idea will underpin everything from the look of your planner or journal to the content, so let yourself and your mind go for it!

Go ahead and dream for a little while, be excited because the journey ahead of you is big and beautiful. Believe in yourself because with a little spark of creativity and some determination, you have got this!

 "Dream big dreams! Imagine that you have no limitations and then decide what's right before you decide what's possible."

— BRIAN TRACEY

BEING CREATIVE

If you are reading this section and you don't identify as a fellow creative then I beg to differ, having the interest in creating your own planner or journal tells me there is creativity within you. It's within everyone. As creative people, a lot of the time we can talk ourselves out of our own ideas. They can be thrown aside as quickly as they manifested in our minds. Largely this can be down to the confidence we hold within ourselves. We never think our ideas are big enough or good enough to be put out into the world. I want to tell you this isn't the truth. Most of the ideas you have will have something amazing in them. Yes, ideas need to be developed but it doesn't mean they can't be worked on, and some ideas aren't right but that does not reflect on your creative ability. Sometimes it's not the right time to bring your idea into the world and that's ok. I'm not saying go against your gut feeling, it's about striking a fine line of falling into the trap of telling yourself the narrative of none of my ideas are good enough to this idea no matter how much I develop it just doesn't feel right.

Top Tip: Keep an ideas book or a notes tab on your phone, we forget our ideas most of the time because we don't write them down. They can pop into our head at any split second, when we are on the bus, or after a good night's sleep. In that moment of inspiration, jot your idea down no matter how small it may seem. Then go back through your book or your phone when you need to get inspired. Looking at your ideas through different eyes on a different day you may see the potential in the smallest thing you have written.

Remember fellow creative, your brain is one of the most amazing things on this planet. The power it holds we will never fully comprehend and the creativity it can birth is phenomenal. You just have to know how to harness and express your creative side. A lot of the time it's our mindset and what we tell ourselves can hold us back. It can affect our confidence and change how we express our true authentic selves. Our mind can create limiting beliefs and tell us things that are not true. We let them hold us back from taking the steps that we know will ultimately help lead to our success. Next time you have thoughts coming into your head that you're not creative enough or your ideas are not good enough, check in and ask yourself are these limiting beliefs? How can I work on them?

I often look for evidence when limiting beliefs come into my head to have proof, they are wrong. You will have had times when your ideas have been great, and you have been successful with what you wanted to achieve. That is proof right there that your ideas are good enough. Don't let your mind hold you back from creating any of your dreams. I know that you are good enough to create anything you want in your future, I believe we are all born to be successful we just have to harness our creativity, our ideas and greatness and act on them. Turn what we can see into reality.

There may be times in this creative project that you may feel stuck, it's a little like writer's block. You might start to feel you don't know how to progress with your project. Any time you experience this leave your project and go and do something fun, listen to music or whatever you need to get your energy back. You will see your project differently after you take some time out.

Anytime you experience feeling stuck then remember this quote, it's one of my favourites and pulls me out of my stuck uninspired self-doubting moments.

 "You can't use up creativity. The more you use, the more you have."

— MAYA ANGELOU

Key points to remember from this section-

- Dream big!
- Don't limit yourself.
- You are creative.
- Your ideas are good enough.
- Believe in yourself and your vision.

Chapter
Two

PLANNING

*I*t's time to get excited about planning your project!

As I mentioned in the introduction, this is such an important phase. It is your time to get really inspired about every detail of your beautiful planner or journal. The next few chapters will break down the planning side of your project, so you don't feel overwhelmed, and you know exactly what you want to achieve.

Getting well planned is really key to a successful project. This is a big project you take on over several months. Project planning is important so you are aware of your deadlines and you can assess your progress as you work through your project.

As you read through each section, try and consider each area over the coming chapters and be honest with yourself. Where are you at and which areas do you need to work on? If you need to work on a couple of areas that's ok, your project might take a little longer but it's worth getting right. I know not everyone who picks up this book is going to have the skills straight away in all areas, for example designing and publishing. I acknowledge there is a lot to learn. Nor will everyone be in the same place in business, you may not have your branding together or even a business. This is ok, a lot of things in business are an evolution project and are always changing. So don't worry if you feel you haven't got everything perfect. In all honesty they probably will never be, no matter how long you've been in business.

I have broken down the basic practical elements you need in your business in this section too. This is to help you if you are looking to start a business off the back of your planner or journal, maybe you still class yourself as very new to the business world. This will give you a foundation to start with that will make your project easier. Ultimately this book is about putting a planner or journal together that is going to benefit your clients and customers and your existing or future business.

Learning new skills as well as developing something really special for your business is an added bonus, even if it does take you a little longer. Don't be disheartened by how long it will take you, put your all into it and enjoy. This is the start of making your dream of having your very own branded planner or journal as part of your business a reality.

Whatever stage you are at go through the planning section, you will need to understand the key integral parts of planning your project. You need a good understanding of your concept and why you are designing your planner or journal.

UNDERSTANDING YOUR PASSION & EXPERTISE

For some of you reading this, your passion will be easily defined. You will know instantly what you are passionate about. For others you will know you want to create a planner or journal but are unsure about where your passion lies. Whichever side of the fence you sit either is ok, this book is for you. Understanding what you're passionate about will give you the driving force to be able to complete your project and ride out the challenging times. Understanding your passion also allows you to explore every possibility and then gets you to niche down in a certain area. This allows your planner or journal to be purposeful and help others with one specific area. Your planner or journal needs to be transformational for the person that is using it. I'm sure you don't want to design a generic planner or journal that is selling in every stationery store. This process is about having a deeper understanding of your passion and purpose and how you are going to help people with your idea. You don't want to solely focus on organisation or planning because every planner or diary has that element. Ask yourself all of these questions.

- What can you specifically help people with?
- What excites and ignites you?
- What inspires you?
- How do you see your planner or journal being used?

To give you an idea of the diverse range you can create with planners and journals, these are some of the people I have helped: Marketing experts, crystal experts, therapists, coaches, NLP practitioners, health and wellbeing practitioners, the list goes on.

No one I have worked with wanted generic planners or journals. They wanted to help their audience in a specific way, so what are you passionate about helping people with?

Maybe you know or maybe you're not sure, keep reading you will figure it out.

Finding your passion goes alongside understanding where your expertise lies. Once you know what you are passionate about and what your expertise are, you can marry the two and come up with a powerhouse of ideas that fit under those umbrellas.

Start by writing a list of everything you love, not just love a little and not because you think you should because everyone else does. I want you to make your list of what fires YOU up on the inside. Ask yourself what do I really love?

Once you have completed your list of passions, write a list of your expertise. Consider everything not just what you think you are good at. Consider what you can talk for hours about, ask others what they think your strengths are, personal and business. What do people ask for your advice on? When you start to consider all of these things you might see yourself in a different light. I can guarantee you are a multi-talented person with several passions and several areas you can consider yourself as an expert. You may see a common thread running through your list or you might not. Still write everything down. If you already have a business, you may have a clearer idea of what your project is going to be about. Still do this exercise, more ideas might jump into your head with different angles you didn't consider before.

Now go back through both lists and see where they meet. Is there a link between what you are passionate about and your areas of expertise? Is there a point where your lists cross over, so you can be passionate about what you are an expert in? This is important because sometimes what we know a lot about we are not necessarily passionate about.

As time goes by and you expand and grow as a person this may change. You will be continuously learning and developing through life. It may be a good idea to repeat this exercise every six to twelve months, this will allow you to develop new ideas and ways to help people with new planners or journals. Remember planners and journals can have lots of editions because you have decided to develop them.

I talk about this because I see people wanting to design an idea because it's on trend rather than them being passionate about it and when you aren't passionate about something it shows. That idea will not gain traction in your business, you will get bored or frustrated and not get your project over the finishing line. Think about your end product when you are marketing it, and if you aren't that passionate about it then your audience is going to be able to tell. You aren't going to sell many copies. I have a belief when we put ideas out into the world it has to come from the right place with the right energy. It's about believing in your product and knowing it will give the right transformation to your customers because it has come from a place of service and wanting to help people live a better life. Your audience will be able to tell if you aren't selling honestly or being genuine and this can do more harm to your business. Understanding what you are passionate about and how you want to help people genuinely is really important.

Completing this exercise will give you the confidence to move forward with your idea. You may also discover something new about yourself. Most of all have fun with it and get really excited because you are about to go on a creative journey.

" "A journey of a thousand miles begins with a single step."

— LAOZI

YOUR TARGET AUDIENCE

Who is your target audience?

If you have a business already and are building your audience or have an existing audience, you are probably already clear on who you are targeting. Still consider who your target market would be when launching your planner or journal, as this can widen your audience. There may be people who are really interested in your publication that you may not have considered before. If you are thinking of launching a business from your planner or journal you will need to give this some thought. Even if you think you have your target audience worked out, sometimes it's great to revisit it. There may be an angle you haven't considered or maybe you need to go more in-depth with this work. Look at a wider audience and who would benefit from your planner or journal, sometimes we need to look at our business from different angles and perspectives to consider something new.

If you don't have a business and you want to start one and this is new to you, then you really have to focus on finding who your target audience is. Be specific. This will help you with getting clarity on your idea and design but also with marketing once you have published or printed your creation.

Don't overcomplicate it, break it down. Who is the person you are wanting to buy your planner or journal? Why would they use it? What problem does your creation solve for them? By doing this work it will benefit your design and marketing. Try to be as detailed as you can but don't let it be a stumbling block, it's better to know something rather than do none of the work. You can always come back to this and keep adding to your list of who your target audience is as it becomes clearer to you.

Here are a few pointers of what you will want to know about your target audience:

- Gender
- Age
- Hobbies & Interests
- Occupation/Salary
- Are they a parent?
- What are their Goals?
- What problem are they facing that needs solving?
- Habits
- Likes/dislikes
- Lifestyle

The main point of the target audience exercise is to understand who you are selling to. Later this will help you design the correct product but also market to the correct people. It will help you write your marketing copy, and it will seem less of a daunting task to sell to your audience because you know who you are selling to, what to say and how to communicate to them. You will know what they need in their life to solve the problem they are facing or create the transformation they are looking for. People connect with stories; you may have a powerful story yourself and this has led you to want to help others through a journal or planner. People will connect with you and your planner and journal more if you share your story. It adds authenticity to you and your brand. If you are struggling with this, try creating a customer avatar. Think of them as an actual person, give them a name even draw them out like a character. Some people are more visual and find it easier to work in this way. There's no right or wrong way of completing this as long as you are clear on your target audience. Remember the more you know about them, the clearer your marketing and targeting will be.

If you come to a complete standstill with this work, go back to your planner or journal idea and dig a little further into who you are helping and why. Going back and doing more work on that stage will help you out later on. Getting really clear on this will help you develop a really in-depth product. Circling back on yourself here may feel like you are taking a step backwards but later on the process will seem easier.

BUSINESS, STARTING OR NONE

You may have a business, or you might be thinking about starting a business or you might have no desire to be a business owner. You can still design your own planner or journal regardless. Either way there are some points for you to consider.

If you have a business start to understand where your planner or journal is going to sit in your business, maybe you have considered this already. Start thinking of your planner or journal as part of your sales funnel. It's a small priced entry level product that allows people to discover you and buy a small piece of what you do to see if they like it. Planners and journals are a great way to appeal to people in the first place because there are a lot of stationery-mad people out there. I should know I am one of them and I'm sure you are too.

The planner industry alone was worth $1.02 billion in 2022. It's big business.

A lot of people only focus on the royalties of sales directly from their planner or journal. Yes, this is important but also, I want you to consider the customer journey. What could a sale of your planner or journal really bring to your business? What if on the back of that one sale, that customer falls in love with everything you do, and buys your online course? Six months later they buy your one to one program. Do you see that one sale can become so much more than the royalty earned from a copy sold?

Your planner or journal can also be a part of your offering in your programs or courses. They make nice gifts, just think how your client would feel receiving a welcome gift from you for signing up for your program. You can up level your programs by offering a VIP package, maybe your planner or journal will be part of the package. There is a possibility of creating returning customers that purchase year after year, because they loved using your creation when they received it as part of your course or program. There are multiple ways your planner or journal can work for you in your business, start thinking outside of the box and don't just focus on copies sold.

This process will strengthen your idea or even change your existing idea completely, but stay with it, it's all part of the journey. The important part is you go on to create something that speaks to your audience and sells.

Over the next few sub chapters I will explain how your planner and journal can work for you from a business perspective and the benefits it can bring to your business. Having a planner or journal as part of your business can have more benefits than just profit. It can help with the growth of your business and brand too.

1. Attracting New Clients

Once you publish your planner or journal it will be available to people all around the world. You may reach people with your planner or journal that you would have never reached on social media. I say this because buying a planner or journal is very different to buying a coaching package or a course. A lot of people will come into your world that might not have otherwise.

Once your customer has purchased your beautiful creation they will be impressed with your content because, you have genuinely helped them. They will want to learn more about you. This is another reason why creating a planner or journal that has a specific transformation for your customer or client is really important. People usually have a problem they are looking to solve or an area they want to improve in their life. For example, if you are a fitness instructor and a healthy eating expert you might create a health and fitness planner with a goals section and a daily calorie tracker. So people can be really specific about what they want to achieve and keep on track. Once that person sees what they can achieve by following your planner they will turn into a social media follower, potentially buying your PT sessions because they want to tone up and improve their fitness further. That's just an example, but people are genuinely curious and want to find out more about you. Especially if you've had a positive impact on them or influenced their life in a positive way.

Always think of the bigger picture. The benefits are more than just profit. What a great benefit to have, new future customers or clients coming into your world and seeing what other products or services you have to offer them. As I mentioned above don't underestimate the power of the customer journey and that your planner or journal can be an incredibly powerful lead magnet. This applies to attracting new people into your audience as well as your existing audience. You will gain more trust with existing audience members that haven't invested in your programs or courses yet. You will find that your audience has natural growth because of your planner or journal. Sometimes people are looking for a small cost item to invest in before the bigger package.

Once your customers find you it is your job to nurture them and convert them into raving fans, purchasing everything you offer. The customer journey can be short, or it can take time for people to buy. It depends on them, but one thing you need to be is consistently showing up with value so they can strengthen their trust in you. Some customers will convert straight away, this is because what you do speaks to them, they get excited and jump in. Some will take time to convert from a cold lead to a warm lead. Everyone's journey is different and some customers will only need to experience your planner or journal and they will be sold on you. Others will need time, sometimes months or even years. Everyone buys on different levels and some people are impulsive or emotional buyers. Some people buy on results and reviews only and that will take time to see and build. Another great point is that you only have to design this content once and it's out there for your audience to purchase.

2. Creating An Additional Income

Producing a planner or journal will create an additional income for your business. You will earn a royalty from each copy sold if you go down the publishing route. This income will be semi passive mostly, it can also be passive, depending on how well your marketing and automation systems are set up and where your planner or journal is placed in your business. When you see how much you can earn per copy sold it may not seem like a lot. Don't let that discourage you, remember it's not only about copies sold but also about bringing new people into your world and showing them what else you have to offer. Think about the customers that will turn into clients and the impact that this will create in your business and your customers worlds. If you add up everything you sell, what profit would you make? If one person came into your business via your planner or journal and purchased everything would your investment be worth it?

Let's now talk about it over the lifetime of your planner or journal. What if you sold only two a day for a year? You would generate a nice additional income. The average royalty is around £5 per copy, some can be more, and some can be less depending on how big your publication is. So, if you sold two copies a day for a year, your income would be £3650. This is only for one year. What if you sold more copies per day or over the year? This is if you used the method of publishing and decided not to do any of the shipping yourself. A print on demand service would print and fulfil your orders, you would just collect the royalties in your bank. Remember don't cap yourself, the impact you could have on the world with one idea is huge. However, you do need a strategy to achieve whatever goal you may set yourself. They won't just fly off the shelf if you do nothing with them.

This is another reason the planning stage is crucial, it allows you to assess where you are now. Do you already have an engaged audience that you can sell to? You want this to be a viable business decision or are you going to build a business off the back of your planner or journal launch? Both are possible just ensure you have your foundations in place. In the past sometimes I've seen people get disappointed when their planner or journal doesn't fly off the shelves quickly, but this is because they haven't got the basics in place, or they weren't clear in their marketing strategy. My services have now developed, and I work through this with my clients, hence why I'm also passing this information on to you. Getting to know your target audience or ideal client well feeds directly into this.

So do you have an existing audience to sell to? If you don't have an audience to sell to, do you know who your target audience is and where to find them?

What strategy can you put in place before you release your planner or journal to gain an audience? I will go into this further later in the book, but I wanted to get you thinking about it for now. The obvious place is social media, make sure you choose the right platform that is going to serve you and your product but most importantly ensure it's where your target audience is. Try and master one or two social platforms. If you've been in business for a while you will know social media is like a full-time job in itself. Be clever with your decisions, you want to be where your target audience is but also you don't want to feel chained to several platforms. Facebook and Instagram have a dual posting facility so only have to post once and it shows up on both platforms, saving you time!

3. Your Existing Audience & Clients

If you have a business that already has the foundations in place, don't forget about your existing audience. These are the people that have already taken the time out to get to know you. Some may have purchased your products and courses. Take time to think about how your planner or journal can help them, what do you already help them with and what value do you already put out there on your business pages?

Can you capture that and turn it into a planner or a journal? When you first release your creation, these are the most likely people that will buy from you because they already know you. The trust is already built and if your planner or journal speaks to them and it's exactly what they want, they are more than likely going to purchase and support you. So when coming up with your planner or journal idea you want to consider your existing audience. If you already have an established business, your planner or journal idea may be really obvious to you. Still go through the planning process so your creation is strong and hits the mark rather than being a weaker version.

Thinking about your existing clients may get your ideas flowing and you may have multiple ideas from working with your clients. This is a great position to be in. Write all your ideas down this may lead to you producing multiple editions of your planner or journal.

Consider if you have any courses or workbooks that help your clients with something specific, can you produce a planner or journal to run alongside your course, that compliments what you already offer? You can enhance your client's experience. Of course, your planner or journal can be used in multiple ways across your business. You can do some market research with your existing audience and clients. Would this add value and how can your offering be the most beneficial to them. This will help you decide where your planner or journal can be placed and if future offerings to your clients and audience can be made stronger by offering your planner or journal as part of a package.

USP

What makes your idea different or unique from other planners and journals available on the market? This is where you will need to consider your USP. When designing a new product, you need to understand what your unique selling point is. What is going to make you stand out from the crowd? Don't think about what you are going to design, think about the experience you can offer your customer and how you are going to make them feel when using your planner or journal. Are you solving a practical problem for your customer or maybe creating a transformation? How is your customer going to benefit by using your publication above anyone else's? What are they going to learn? Maybe your topic of expertise doesn't currently offer a planner or journal format. If your area of expertise does offer a planner or journal have a look around. What is making the best sellers sell and are you offering anything different or in addition? I don't believe that there's too many planners or journals on the market because they all offer something different. Whether that is practicality, content, how the planner or journal is used or the aesthetics. Some people buy on just athletics alone, but you don't want to base your creation solely on this. Focus on how is it going to change your customers life once they start using it? I know you might think that's a little dramatic for the use of a planner or journal but take a moment to think about how we buy. We all buy when we make an emotional connection or, when we are given a solution to something that is causing us a problem within our lives. Knowing your ideal customer and your target market is essential before you figure out what your USP is. Without being really specific on who your audience is and who you are creating your journal or planner for you won't be specific enough with your USP.

One thing that stops people in their tracks from designing their planner or journal is thinking that the market is too saturated. Yes, the market is busy, but you haven't got your branded planner or journal out there. If you do all the in-depth work before you start, you will realise how special your idea is. You will start to understand that you have the power to design anything you want to help others, wouldn't the world be better off with your planner or journal in it? Another thing that sets you apart is YOU! You're unique, how you write your content, how you communicate and how you design. No one has the exact same ideas and even if they did, they would execute them differently. If you run a service-based business where you work directly with your clients, you will already know the importance of selling brand you. Being the face and brand of your business can be challenging but in all honesty it's what sets you apart from other businesses in the same field. Think about everything about you, your business, your brand, your planner or journal. What is the unique selling point?

With a big offering out there of planners and journals, you may feel your idea has already been created however, there is room for every idea. As I have mentioned above you will put your own unique stamp on that idea and make it unique to you and your business. Do some market research but ensure this isn't going to influence what you design. Remember you don't want to copy any ideas. Try and be objective and treat it as a fact-finding exercise. Have a look to see if there are any gaps in the market that you can fill? You never know what you will find until you conduct some research. If your planner or journal idea is already on the market, how can you make yours different? What angle can you give to your idea to make it different? What added benefits can you give to your idea? Don't see it as a bad thing, it proves there is a market already there. Give yourself permission to create something even better get your idea pumped so it's bigger and better than the version already created.

PHYSICAL PRACTICALITIES

It's easy to fall into the trap of wanting to throw everything into your creation. Making it the all-singing and dancing planner or journal of all time. However, a well-thought-out planner or journal structure will make your content stand out. You want to make your planner or journal easy to use for your customer. There is no point in overcomplicating it. You don't want your customers throwing your creation to the back of the cupboard only after using it a couple of times because they are frustrated with it. No one wants to be confused. The point of someone buying a planner is usually to be more organised with an area of their life, people are looking for structure, continuity and simplicity. They want to make their life easier. So, give them that in the area you specialise in, they want to learn from you. Sometimes there are exceptions to this rule. For example, if you wanted to create a two in one planner and journal and have both together in one publication. This is ok, you are giving your customer the opportunity to plan, learn, structure and emotionally develop all in one space. You will also need to think about the size of your publication. You want to be clear on how someone is going to use your planner or journal if they picked it up for the first time. Does your customer need to be able to travel around with it easily or is it a desk publication? Consider the thickness. My advice here would be to try to keep your creation below 400 pages if you want your planner or journal to be carried around easily. Over this your planner or journal will become heavy and chunky, your customer will give up using it and find something else. If it is a desk publication you are looking to design, you can design up to 600 pages when publishing.

Journals need to be laid out clearly so your customer knows how to use it, are you going to introduce prompts? It's a good idea to add a page near the front on how to use your journal with any instructions your customer needs to follow to get the best experience. Again, your customer is looking for help in their life, make things clear for them.

Clear divided sections are another way to make your planner or journal user friendly, if you choose the publication route you aren't going to be able to add physical dividers. You need to get creative on how you are going to create separate sections throughout your planner or journal, making it easier to use for your customer. The way you can do this is through design. Try and think of ways you could design your planner or journal to incorporate this feature. Your customer wants a clear-cut product that will solve their problem. You want to avoid your customer feeling overwhelmed. Think about separate title pages so it creates the divide from section to section in your planner or journal. Colour coding the edge of the pages can also be another way to create dividers and sections. Depending on the content and how your publication is laid out, think about having page numbers and a contents page. This isn't for all planners and journals and can make it more confusing in some, decide what is right for you. If you have a lot of sections or written content this is something, you may want to consider. Making planner tab stickers for the edge of the pages can be another tip to create the dividers. You would have to ask a printer to make these for you. If you are choosing to go down the printing route you will be able to have dividers with tabs, so you won't need to consider this. If you are choosing the publishing route, take time to consider all these options. You could also sell the sticker tabs as an extra product alongside your planner or journal.

DESIGN PRACTICALITIES

We have already covered the practical side and the usability for your customer. In this section, you will need to consider the design practicalities elements like the size, including dimensions as well as page count. This will be mainly influenced by how you want your customer to use your planner or journal as discussed in the physical practicalities section. However, you need to consider other outcomes too in terms of design. If you are having your design professionally printed how much will the size, you would like cost? This is the time to research. If the cost is too high then find a solution, maybe you cut your page count down or pick a smaller page size. There is also the option of picking a budget paper. Contact a printer and see where you can cut down on costs, choosing elements like the type of binding and foiling the front cover will increase the cost. If you are going to publish your design, check that you can publish in the size you have chosen to design in. In general, with publishing, you can get a variety of sizes. Custom design sizes are allowed if you wanted a specific size but only within certain measurements. These can be found on the KDP website.

How will your planner or journal flow? Creating flow in a planner or journal is integral for the customer, it's not only about content but the flow of the design. Your customer is going to open and use this every day. It needs to be beautifully designed as well as practical. Here are some tips on how you can create the flow in your planner or journal. When you are designing what will your style be? Will it be minimalist, or do you want more energy flowing through the design than that? Thinking about your design can bring up multiple questions with the practical side of things. You need to think about where your customer needs to write in your journal or planner and not fill these spaces with design. The backgrounds of pages you can fill with images, colour and designs. A great way not to overwhelm your customer with design is to turn down the opacity, making your design slightly more transparent to give a more tonal quality. You have to give acknowledgement to the design on each page and ensure each page flows into the next. Imagine flicking through a planner or journal and getting really harsh pages that stand out every so often. Then you know you have pages that don't compliment the rest of your design. You don't want to aim for that, you want your design to be coherent and compliment all the way through your planner or journal. Experiment with different design styles, you may already have a specific style and that's great - go with that, because that will be unique to you. If you don't have a design style play around and find out who you are as a designer and have fun with it, then assess it for the practicalities we have talked about.

Something else to consider is whether your planner will be dated or undated? This question comes up all the time and it is something you need to think about and consider. There are pros and cons to each.

Dated planners only have a short shelf life and that is not a full year. When you launch your dated planner, you will want to launch that around September. This gives your customers enough time to get prepared to purchase their new year planners. The shelf life of a dated planner is around six to eight months including the pre-sale period. There will be people that don't mind missing a month or two because they found you late or they were disorganised. After this time planners for the current year are discounted. The great thing about dated planners is that your customers don't have to write in their own dates. Having a dated planner also allows you to update it every year. This can be looked at as an expense, but it can also be looked at as a fresh opportunity, to update the design and theme. Because of the redesign element of a dated planner, it is less passive and turns into a yearly project. Maybe this is what you are looking for, and something to consider if you wanted to rebrand your planner every year anyway. Releasing different editions or refreshing the look of your planner every year can work in your favour and drive sales. You will have the customers that bought from you the previous year as well as new people that have discovered your business throughout the year and through the launch phase of your new edition. Because your planner will have a start date, your audience knows if they don't buy it, they will miss out, causing the excitement and driving sales.

An undated planner will have a lifetime as long as your business. With only the need to redesign if you want to change the theme or colour scheme of your planner. If you brand your planner the same as your business this change will only need to happen if you rebrand your business. This makes this option more passive. Your customers can come across your product at any time of the year and will be able to use it. The only downside is that your customers will have to write their own dates. Some people will see this as a negative, but a lot of people will overlook this factor if the other content of the planner is just what they've been looking for. Another positive factor is that your clients and customers can start using your planner straight away, at whatever point of the year they discover you, they don't have to wait until 1st January.

Now you know the pros and cons of dated and undated planners, you need to think about what is best for your business and your customers. Do some market research here and ask what your audience would like. Put a poll on your social media pages and see which is the more popular option. Get some real feedback and opinions, this will help you design the right planner for your audience.

There is nothing stopping you from designing one of each. This gives you the option to design a dated one every year without the pressure, if you didn't get around to the redesign you would still have the undated option to fall back on. This also allows your audience to choose and you to see which is the most popular in your business. Everyone has different preferences and is hard to cater for all but if you didn't want to minimise your options create both!

BRANDING

Whilst you are planning your project this is the perfect time to consider your branding. You may already have your branding perfectly mapped out and you are ready to go. This opportunity may give you the chance to tidy up your branding for your business especially if you feel you have been winging it until this point. It may even inspire you to totally rebrand. How your planner or journal is designed can make or break it. You don't have to brand your planner or journal exactly the same as your business, you can create a whole new concept for your planner or journal, but you would want something to complement your business. You need a cohesive brand idea so your planner or journal will look amazing. It's about minimising fonts and colours, choosing the right colours and making a cohesive design so it has impact. It's the difference of it looking professional or amateur.

Branding is about communication; ensure everything you choose communicates what your brand stands for. Knowing the key points about your business, your target audience and your values will influence your choices when putting your branding together. You can go into your branding in a lot of depth, however this book will touch on the key points, allowing you to consider the basics and create a beautiful brand package. Where do you start with your branding? A good place to start is to understand your brand's values, what does your brand stand for? If you know what your brand stands for, this will influence the colours and images used and how the design looks. For example, if your brand represents sustainability then the likely hood is you will be looking at natural or woodland colours. Having an understanding of this will get you to a clearer place before you move on to mood boards and branding templates. If you are the face of your business, you and everything you stand for will be your brand. Pick colours and images that reflect you, your values and your personality.

Choosing colours is always a fun job. A lot of people choose their brand colours because they like them, rather than understanding that colours evoke emotions and make people feel a certain way. Either attracting them to your business or pushing them away. Colour can also influence how people think and the reactions we have in our bodies. Colours can also portray different things in different cultures and parts of the world. For example, in the Western World red means excitement, danger and love, in the Eastern World red means luck, long life and happiness. Having a basic understanding and awareness of colour is essential when you are designing.

It is also good to keep in mind where your audience is based, a lot of online businesses have a worldwide audience.

There are so many different ways you can use colour; you can go really in depth with colour psychology. But understanding a little about colour will help you to communicate your brand and business effectively. You can access colour wheels online that will tell you what each colour and shade of colour means. For example, green and its shades are a cold colour palette it represents money, new beginnings, growth and abundance, it can also represent jealousy and a lack of experience. Whilst brown can add a sense of trust, reliability and unity to your design. It can balance a design and also make you relax. Understanding colour will allow you to communicate your brand and define how you want to be seen and stand out. You want to be able to connect with your audience and allow your audience to connect with you. They want to know in an instant if they resonate with what you are putting out there. We see marketing images all the time, you want to stand out in a positive way to capture people's attention. Remember the power of asking people what they think? If you have colours or imagery that you can't decide on, ask your audience or a group of people that would fit into your target audience demographic. This will allow you to understand if you are communicating correctly and if your audience understands your message. Don't forget about your wider audience too. Feedback is a massive tool and one that will change your business.

Creating a colour palette can take hours, especially when you are trying to take into consideration all of the points mentioned above. Brand values, colour psychology and effectively communicating. A good colour palette contains around five to six different colours that contrast or complement each other. Creating a colour palette allows you to find out the hex or RGB code for each colour. This is the code that is assigned to a specific colour and allows you to create your design using your colour palette, by using this code, your colours will be exactly correct. You can change your colours palette on Canva and Affinity with hex codes. Hex codes allow you to do the same thing as RGB codes, but they are structured differently on some design suites you can use both.

How do you create a colour palette? Some of you will know the type of colours you want to have as part of your brand and some of you won't. That's ok, if you have an idea, I suggest going on to a free website called Coolors. This will allow you to play around with colours and shades to create your own palette. You can download the hex or the RGB codes on your PDF. Export your palette once you have found the colours you would like to use, and then you have your codes ready to add to your brand board.

If you are starting from scratch look around for inspiration starting from nothing is really exciting. It gives you the chance to consider everything with fresh eyes and all the points we have talked about so far. Giving you the opportunity to create a strong message with your branding from the start.

Other ways you can put a colour palette together is creating a mood board. Mood boards are a great way to find inspiration but also ensure you find the correct tone and mood you want to create. Once you have your pictures you can depict colours and shades from those pictures building your brand colour palette, the website Coolors has a tool you can use to take colours from a picture or a photo. You can create your mood board digitally or by cutting and sticking pictures and photos of inspiration out of glossy magazines. It just depends on how you want to be creative and what feels right for you.

There is no right or wrong way of getting your colour palette together, these are some ideas of how to start that process.

The next part of the branding journey is to consider what fonts to use. There are so many fonts to choose from, when you go into the world of fonts you can feel bombarded. Aim to choose around three fonts but no more than four, and at least one that is a normal paragraph text. If you would like a calligraphy-type font, please test a few out. It's not until you use them, you see they are hard to read or how easy they are to misread. Try to minimise the number of fonts you use because you want your design to look clean and fresh, you don't want it to look all over the place. An effective way to use fonts is to use your more stylish fonts for headings and quotes and your plainer fonts for subheadings and paragraphs. You can set which fonts you are going to use on your brand board. You can follow this to give you continuity throughout your planner or journal. A great way to look for different fonts is on Pinterest. Pin the ones you love and make a note of the names so you can purchase them. Creative Market is also a great source for fonts. Here you can download singular fonts or packs and they are an inexpensive way of building up your font library. Of course, whatever design suite you decide to use will have fonts already available. However, if you do want something a little different or specific, building up your own font library is a good idea. All fonts you purchase can be uploaded to Canva and used with the Affinity design suite. Most of all have fun, pick something that really communicates your message and makes you stand out from the crowd.

If you are buying or downloading imagery or fonts, please select the appropriate licencing for the product. If you don't there could be legal consequences if you publish, print or sell with incorrectly licensed products. Please double-check everything.

Do you have a logo? It is recommended that you have a logo so you can print it on your finished publication. If you have a business this will not be new to you. A logo allows your brand to stand out and to be easily identified. This will be a part of how your business and your brand will build recognition, trust and reputation. Logos are best if they are easily recognisable, you don't have to complicate them. A lot of businesses have two logos, a main logo and a sub mark logo. The sub mark logo is a simplified version of the main logo. This is used when the main logo can't be displayed because the space may be too small and the main logo becomes unrecognisable. The sub mark logo can be an image or a simple mark without text, it could be just the first letters of your business name. This can then be printed or published in the bottom corner of the back cover of your planner or journal.

To make your branding clear and concise use a brand template, you can download one of these for free on The Printable Life website, scan the code below-

Brand Board Template

www.theprintablelife.enlitly.com/site/squeeze1

You will be able to edit your brand board in Canva for free.

This will allow you to display your logo, colours, fonts, mood board and any other information you want to include. These are only the basics of branding, if you know more about branding and want to go more in depth then please develop this further. If you are new to branding don't get overwhelmed and as I always say, keep it simple.

Once you have developed your branding you may want to consider protecting it. I can't give you any legal advice here as I am not trained to do so but I would like to point out to you the benefits of trademarking your business name and logo. Trademarking gives you added protection with your business name and brand so no one else in the same industry can use it. If you don't then you run the risk of someone else using your name and trademarking it. Which will leave you needing to rebrand everything you have created including your planner or journal. This means more cost and time you have to invest in starting everything again. Please do some research. If you are outside of the UK, laws may be different. It is your responsibility to protect your own business. Have a look at how many countries you need to register your trademark in and which categories you will need to be registered in. The more categories and countries you need it becomes more expensive. It is worth it because changing your whole business could be just as or even more costly. If you are in the UK, you can apply for a trademark yourself through the government website or use a third-party company to fill in the paperwork on your behalf. Going through another company will have additional costs.

It's not just about cost, it's also about protecting what you have created. You have put your heart and soul into your business as well as your products including your planner and journal. Do your research and protect your business in relation to the laws of the country where you are based.

Key points to remember from this section-

- Plan, Plan, Plan!
- Get inspired and understand your passions and expertise.
- Understand who your target audience is and your USP.
- Be clear on the usability of your planner or journal, remember it's about your customer.
- Tidy up or create your branding.
- Look into trademarking.

Chapter
Three

DESIGN

*D*esigning is the fun part. This is where you see your creative planning come to life from your lists to all its beauty. Taking your scribbles and ideas from the planning stage and seeing your idea start to become real, it's such a magical moment. As you go through this section, I point out what to consider in your design and give you tips along the way. If you are brand new to graphic design, you will have to pick skills up as you move through your project. This will of course add time on to your project, but it will be valuable for future projects and essential for this one.

There's many people out there thinking you need fancy expensive design suites. When in fact that's not true at all. You can design planners or journals using free tools and online design suites that you pay for on a subscription basis. That's the exciting part you don't need to spend a lot on the initial outlay if you are willing to put in the amount of time needed to complete the design work yourself. Having completed planner and journal projects for clients at The Printable Life™, I can give you an honest answer of how long a project can take. This is around 50 hours of design time spread over 12 weeks, some projects can be more. It does depend on what depth you are wanting to take your design. If you want to design a lined journal that is going to take less time than a 12 month planner. If you want to design a journal that is prompted and every page is different, that is going to take more time than a planner. It is a huge commitment, and this is why the planning section was crucial.

BEFORE YOU START DESIGNING

If you are new to designing before you start, decide which design suite you are going to use. If you are unsure a lot of the online design suites offer a free trial. It's best to try a few out and see which one you like the best. There will be one that you will gel with more than others, it could be as simple as you prefer the layout of one rather than another. Some are overwhelming with multiple menus of tools and effects. It's important you feel comfortable using the basic tools for example page setup, lines, shapes, fill tool and text. If you play around with these then you can build your skills up as time goes on. I don't want you to get down with the technicality of designing if you don't have the basics in place. You will be able to complete your project but, you have to lay your foundations first, so take one step at a time. Be honest with yourself, where are your skills in terms of designing? Do you need to learn how to use the design suite you have chosen? Maybe you haven't even chosen what design suite you are going to use and that's ok. I'll make some suggestions in this chapter. If you're stuck it may help you choose. It's just a case of putting the time in to get the reward if you are new to the world of graphic design.

Before we talk about design programs, I want you to ask yourself what are you familiar with and what level of skill you have. There's no right or wrong answer to this question, but please be honest with yourself. There are programs you can use to make it slightly easier for you if you are a beginner. You might already be a pro with several design suites and that's great, you can take your pick. If you are a beginner to intermediate-level designer, I recommend Canva as a great starting point. You can use the free version or sign up for the pro version, this version gives you loads of extra features. It's clear, easy to use and you can pick up the basics in Canva very fast. If you decide to use the free version, you will not be able to use the advanced features. Some of these features include resizing documents and converting your document into CMYK format, this is the colour palette that you need for professional printing and publishing. The monthly subscription to Canva Pro is inexpensive so even if you use it only for the duration of this project, it may be worth investing. You will know what is right for you and make the right decision.

If you are an intermediate-level designer and don't want to use Canva, have a look at the Affinity suite, publisher is great for planner and journal design.

If you already have previous experience with other design suites then, there is no point learning another design package and starting from scratch. Use what you know.

I know what you are thinking, you're not sure how I can teach you design skills from a book. Well, I'm not going to. I am going to give you the method of how I design planners and journals so you can apply this to your design. This is about thinking in simple minimalist design terms and paying close attention to detail and layout. A smart planner or journal is eye catching and beautiful, you can tell even if one thing is out of line. Everything needs to be on point so it will look professional. Designing planners and journals simplistically is more effective. This doesn't mean you can't add your brand touches, your personality or a little design flare. You just need to find a way to add this without swamping the entire design in Clipart and making it look crowded. Think about how you are going to apply your style and your flare to your planner or journal without going crazy and making it not user friendly.

Remember to minimise your font choices to three to four as mentioned earlier. There can be a desire to get carried away and use lots of different fonts, colours and illustrations. Generally, for fonts the following is a great basis to work from, using different fonts for each category.

- Title / heading fonts
- Subtitle fonts
- Paragraph or main body fonts
- Quote or title page fonts

The cleaner the layout and design of your planner or journal will not only add a more professional look but will be clearer for your customer to navigate and use. You don't want to confuse your customer and make the layout overcrowded so it's difficult to fill out. If you have followed the planning section, you will have been looking at other journals and planners for inspiration. The layout of these will have similarities. Getting the layout perfect is really important, and yes you can break away from what you see in other planners or journals. You don't have to have a goals section or a to do list if that isn't relevant to you.

Before we get started going through the design method, you need to consider the page setup. You will need to decide on your trim size. This is the size of your planner or journal once published and printed. You will need to go to the Amazon KDP website for your margins and bleed measurements. This will be different for all publications depending on your page count. If you are using a traditional printer, please check with them to see what your measurements need to be. Once you have made the calculation, create the size of your page in whichever design program you have decided to use. In Canva you will have to place your margin lines on the page. You can snap margin lines in place by dragging them from the ruled areas. Canva is less precise, but it's still a great program to use. Affinity you can set margin lines when you set up the page. These will show automatically and be specific to the measurements you input. If you do miss calculate you can go back later and change the page setup however, it does turn into a more time-consuming job, because you will have to alter your design too. It's best to get it correct, first time.

Top Tip: Try and do a rough calculation of the number of pages you will design. For example, if you are going to design a planner with a week over two pages that's 104 pages, plus your 12 month title pages, 20 notes pages, 50 journal pages and 1 introduction page. That's a total of 187 pages. Check on Amazon KDP if you are near the cut-off point to change your margin sizes.

THE L.A.S.T METHOD

When you start looking at the layouts of a planner or a journal, it seems complicated from a design perspective. Especially when you are faced with designing your own. All the way through this book you will see a common thread and that is simplicity. As you know I like to break things down and not overcomplicate anything. This doesn't mean you can't have a complex design, but it does mean you don't need to over complicate your approach. If your design is complex for your main week or day planner pages, I would suggest sketching it out on paper first. This is so you know exactly what you are designing when you sit in front of the computer, and you can ensure there are enough boxes and places for all of your content.

The L.A.S.T method was created from how I see planner and journal design myself. I based this on how I could explain this type of design to someone else. I know what I am looking for in my head, but I wanted to teach you too.

L.A.S.T stands for:

Lines

Alignment

Shapes

Text

Now look back over the planners and journals you were looking at for inspiration. You will notice throughout the design, it's all made up of these four things. Breaking the design right down makes it a simpler task. When I look at designs now this is what I see, lines, alignment, shapes and text. Like a technical drawing. It's seeing through the product to the technical side, which isn't that technical when broken down into the L.A.S.T method.

How can you make your design your own? By using this method, but also not being scared to break the rules, remember you want an element of simplicity with your own edge of personality. There are several ways you can do this. Adding colour, you can add accents of colour to boxes, titles, lines, highlighting text and underlining text. You can add faded background textures or patterns and so much more.

Lines– Lines will make up most of your planner or journal. When you are drawing using a design suite you need to ensure that your lines are straight. Avoid adjoining lines crossing over at the point where they meet. This is something to check if you are designing a planner because you will have drawn your own diary templates. If you have drawn anything in your design, please check it. I know this sounds basic but getting the basics right will be the difference between an end product looking rough around the edges and a polished design. To ensure your lines meet at the adjoining points, make use of the zoom in tool. Lines need to be of the correct thickness. If they are too heavy your planner or journal will look less slick, you will know when looking at your design if you need to change this. The colour of the lines is another thing to bear in mind. Don't use too light colours. Remember most of your pages are going to be white so you will want a colour that will stand out. If you want to pick paler colours still, choose paler colours that contrast with the white page and you can see.

Alignment- This part is tricky and most time consuming. When you have everything in alignment it makes your design pop. Ensuring everything is lined up correctly will give you the sharpest planner or journal. Pay attention to shapes and bullet points and in particular continuing boxes across pages for example, if diary pages are split across two pages, then they need to line up. Make use of the automatic alignment tools, watch for these on your screen. They will tell you when you are in line with other elements on the page. When drawing lines, make sure they are straight, all design packages will show you the angle tool when drawing. Pay close attention to detail, are bullet points aligned and spaced equally apart? Ensure your spacing between lines and boxes are equal, especially on notes sections.

Shapes- Shapes can be used to create boxes or points of interest throughout your planner or journal. You don't have to stick to squares or rectangles you can choose different shapes, depending on where you are placing them. What would you like your customer to use them for? Remember the usability aspect I talked about in a previous chapter. Always ask yourself, does this create the space needed so the person using this planner or journal can write what they need to? When designing the layout space is tight and you have to be clever in how you design each page. Consider every detail with the shapes you choose to use including the placement. Even down to if you are going to choose rounded edges or squared edges. Everything adds to the aesthetic. Shapes can be used to create boxes to write in as well as create features such as bullet points. You don't have to stick to traditional shapes you can play around, maybe use hearts or diamonds instead of squares and circles.

Text- I mentioned earlier when I talked about branding that you don't want to choose more than four fonts. You also want to ensure that the fonts you choose complement each other and look good together. Have fun and play around with this. The size of text is important too, make sure you have continuity throughout your planner or journal. You can do this by ensuring your headings are all in one font and the same size.

Same with subtitles, paragraph or body text, quotes and title pages.

 "Fast is fine, but accuracy is everything".

— WYATT EARP

BASE PAGES

If you are designing a planner rather than a journal, keep in mind you are not going to design every single page. Once you have designed what I call the base pages you can duplicate them and edit dates if needed. Be clever with your time after all this project is going to take you many hours, so work smarter with your time. If you can reuse layouts or duplicate them this will save you a lot of time. Make a plan and understand which pages you only have to design once. Journals are a little different. If you are going to design a journal that has different questions on each page, then you will have to design each page. There is no duplication process or base pages unless you have a lined notes section. If there are writing pages that are all identical in your journal you will only have to design them once and then duplicate them throughout the journal.

The average planner is around 300 pages long whereas a journal can range from 150 to 300 pages. If you can save some precious time by duplicating pages take that opportunity.

Examples of base pages in a planner:

Dairy pages

Notes pages

Review or reflection pages

Examples of base pages in journals:

Journal writing pages

Notes pages

Any exercises that you want to duplicate throughout the journal e.g.- selfcare pages.

DEVELOPING YOUR DESIGN

Your design will change several times from your first draft to printing and publishing. This is essential, it's how you take your design to the next level. There may not be much to change but, as you go through this process you will start to pay attention to the detail. If you are a perfectionist like me then this is where you will spend hours obsessing over everything. If you haven't got an eye for detail either try or go over your design with a keen eye. Or if you know someone who is a perfectionist let them have a look and give you feedback.

For this process you need to look at your design from a distance too, objectively and through fresh eyes. Do the fonts complement each other? Does the planner or journal flow in the content and design? Do you need to move the order around so your customers or clients can use it better? Do your colours complement each other and have you used them well? There are so many things you need to put under the microscope at this stage and it can feel a little frustrating but, I can honestly say it's worth it. Again, this is what will take your design from a nice design to a fabulous and professional design. When I work with my clients, I offer three reviews as part of my design packages, and this is where the transformation happens. It allows you to dig deep into the detail and scrutinise your design.

I would recommend doing this process at least three times. Ensure you are taking a break every couple of days between each review session so you can look at your design through fresh eyes.

Once you are happy with your overall design you can move on to duplicating your base pages if needed.

FORMATTING AND DOWNLOADING YOUR DESIGN

This is where you want to make sure everything is formatted correctly. Ensure the headings are all the same font and size along with the paragraphs, sub-paragraphs, quotes and divider section pages. Continuity through your design is crucial. You need to check your alignment and that everything is within the margin lines. It's really the final check before you download your design, so you are happy with everything.

Top Tip: Change the page view to a grid-style view so you can see pages side by side. This is an easy way of checking that page's line up, as a preliminary check. You might still have to make amendments later.

Remember to read through for spelling and punctuation mistakes, it's an easy check to forget.

Once all of your formatting checks have been completed, and everything is in the order you would like, there are a couple of formatting steps you need to do before downloading your manuscript ready for printing or publishing.

1. Download your file in PDF print.
2. Convert your file to a CMYK colour format.

You need to have your file in a CMYK format for the printing process, professional printers use a CMYK palette. An RGB palette is used for digital design and is most probably what you have used for your planner or journal design. If you publish or print an RGB file the colours you have used will be off they may be brighter or duller either way your design won't look the same, don't worry this is easy to convert. If you are using Canva when you go to download your print PDF, you will also have the option further down to change the colour palette to CMYK, then download your file.

If you are not using Canva and have used Affinity, you can convert the document if you haven't already into a CMYK palette before you download it to PDF print. These settings will be found in document setup. If you haven't used either of these programs and can't convert your document in the design suite you have used, you can convert your PDF using Adobe Acrobat. To use this, you will have to pay a subscription fee, there is a free trial included.

I know this might sound a little technical, make a note of this step because it is important and come back to it when you need to. Don't let anything hold you back, take each step one step at a time and break it down.

COVER DESIGN

After designing the inside of your planner, it's time to design the cover. This is where you start to see your design come together and see what your planner or journal will look like. Do some research about what makes a great cover. If you are going down the publishing route, then have a look on Amazon at the published planners or journals, see which ones sell best and take note of the cover design. This is not to copy but to look at what makes the cover stand out. Is it the use of colour, font, imagery or layout? There will be a lot to look at, don't get blindsided, again this is for inspiration and research purposes. Don't compare yourself, you are creating something unique to you, but it is always good to look at what is selling. I'm not suggesting you need to design your cover exactly the same. I want you to understand what attracts people, covers usually have a certain feel about them. Something that appeals to your audience. Remember people buy with an emotional connection. Whether you portray that through imagery, colours or words. The online marketplace is vast, so you have to stand out from your competition.

People only have a thumb-nail to see your cover online and that's the point where they will choose if they want to click to find out more and potentially purchase. Think about how you can make your cover stand out so they want to click on your product to find out more. Bold and simple stands out, so it doesn't mean throw everything at the cover. However think about how you are going to use your colours, fonts, imagery and the placement. You could choose to use a contrasting colour on the cover. Pay attention to what your vision was, will it get noticed online?

Once you have completed your research or if you already have a cover in mind, then you will be ready to design. If you are using a printers, please check your specifications with them before you design your cover. If you are using Amazon KDP to publish you can use the KDP cover calculator. This will allow you to type in all of your specifications and download a cover template. The template will give you overall dimensions. Use these to set up your page in a separate design document. You will see on the template there are red borders. Your text can not go outside of these lines otherwise it will be cut off when printed. Once you have designed your cover, upload the KDP template to your design suite and overlay it on your design. Alter the transparency of the template so you can see your design through it but still see the lines on the template. This is how you check your design is within the red lines. Once you are happy with your design, delete the Amazon template, so only your design is left on the screen. Remember to download your cover as a PDF print document and in the palette CMYK.

Key points to remember from this section-

- Choose a design package to use.
- Get to know the basic functions if it is new to you.
- Use the L.A.S.T method to help you design your planner or journal.
- Ensure your page setup is correct with trim, margin and bleed measurements.
- Develop and review your design.
- Duplicate base pages.
- Format and prepare for downloading.
- Download as a print to PDF document in a CMYK palette.
- Design your cover.

Chapter
Four

PUBLISHING

Why Use Publishing?

There are so many benefits to publishing your journal or planner and I know I have touched on some of these throughout this book. However, this section will explain everything in more detail.

Publishing your planner or journal is a great option if you don't have a big budget for printing. The way print-on-demand publishing works is you upload your design. When a customer purchases your publication, the print-on-demand publisher will print that copy and dispatch it. This means no stock storage or postage costs for you. Imagine having to pay for storage because you have hundreds of planners or journals to store. Or risking storing them in your garage where they could get damaged. It takes all of those stresses, worries and costs away. There's no minimum order from a print-on-demand publisher. If there is a mistake in your planner or journal and you haven't noticed it until you have ordered the printed version, don't worry. You can edit your file and re-upload it at any time and you haven't had to order 500 copies from a printer to notice the mistake. Any amendments you make to your design will take 72 hours to go live once Amazon has approved your file.

There are several companies out there that you can use, the one I have experience with is Amazon KDP. Amazon pays you royalties every time you sell a copy. The amount will vary from each publication depending on how expensive it is to print, the colour you have used and the total page count. These elements always effect how much Amazon will pay you. Once you have set your price Amazon will pay you the same royalty amount per copy. This is one reason why in previous chapters I mentioned not going over 400 pages. The average royalty amount is around £5 per copy. I've designed some planners and journals that have been £10 and some only £2, so there is a big variation.

If you are looking for a bigger profit margin there is another way you can use Amazon, however this doesn't eliminate having to store your planners or journals in your spare room or the delivery charges and fulfilment. When you publish your planner or journal on Amazon you can then order author copies, these are copies of your publication that you as the author can purchase at the printing cost, you can order from one up to up to 999 copies at a time. The average printing cost I have seen is around £10 as I mentioned above this can vary. You can purchase your author copies and then sell your planner or journal through your website and social media. If you sell your publication for £25 excluding postage, you have made £15 profit rather than the Amazon royalty. It also depends on if you want to have the responsibility of the postage and packaging, or if you want a more passive way of selling your planner or journal. For now, keep your options open if you haven't decided.

The downsides to Amazon KDP are: It's a book printing service this means if you would like any extra features in your planner or journal, KDP will not be able to provide these. We need to be realistic here, if you want to go for the ultimate dream and have the dividers, gold spiral binder, a beautiful box and foiling, you need to use a printers Amazon isn't going to be right for you. Even though the planner or journal with all the special features may be the ultimate dream, there can be steps you need to take to get there. Maybe what Amazon offers can help you achieve that, especially if you don't have the budget right now to invest in printing. Can you release a first edition of your planner using KDP or maybe a budget version of your planner or journal? This will give you the opportunity to go all in practically risk-free and allow you to raise funds for your ultimate version. You can invest in printing in the future and achieve your bigger vision. As I have said before there are ways to work around barriers. You will achieve your big dream; you just need to take the appropriate steps to get there. If you can invest in the printing and all of the luxury features go for it!

If you're not completely sold on the publishing concept, still upload your design and order a proof and see your design in real life. It would be great to see if your design is working on paper and this is an inexpensive way of doing that, it may even change your mind. Print-on-demand services offer an amazing outcome and it blows me away each time my client receives their planner or journal, the excitement and joy I see on their faces is amazing.

USING A PRINTERS

Printing is the option for you if you want specific features as I mentioned before. I want you to understand that printing is a big investment with risk attached to it. Yes, this is about business and risk is attached to everything, but we can always minimise and take calculated risks. If you have the budget and your business has a big audience already, this will be a no brainer for you. You probably will want to go all in. Just be aware that at the printing stage you need to ask for a sample, so you can check everything to ensure your design and content is correct and the quality is what you are expecting. Remember once you have committed to printing 500 copies plus there's no going back, even if you see a mistake after they have been printed. Ensure you see pictures of the printer's past work or even better if you know they have worked with a specific company, order one of their planners, journals or notebooks so you can have a look at the quality of the printing. You don't want to commit to an investment if the quality is lacking. Be clear about your specifications, have a think about what features you would like and if they are all necessary. Every feature you add, you will pay extra for. If you do want the extra features and the luxury version most printers will outsource this work to manufacturers in Asia. If cutting down on cost is what you are looking for, do some research and see if you can directly contact a manufacturer. This can come with huge risks; you don't have a relationship built with the manufacturer like the printing company will. You don't have proof of the quality of their work.

My advice would be to research, see if they can provide photos of their past work. Is there any reviews from real clients or customers? It is safer to use a printers, even if they are going to outsource the work, they will have experience with the manufacturers they use. It's your choice to make and I know you will make the right decision for you and your project. If you see your planner or journal as a printed version rather than a published version there are ways you can get around the cost. You can put your planner or journal on pre-sale, to sell them to your customers before they are printed, in promise they will be one of the first people to obtain your planner or journal by a certain date. This way you can fund or part-fund your first print run. If you don't have a big enough audience to do this then, build your audience. You need to get in front of more people which can take time.

CHOICES ON AMAZON KDP

Amazon do offer a range of choices which are really good when it comes to creating your beautiful planner or journal. You can choose from-

- Paperback.
- Hardcover.
- Glossy or matte cover finish.
- Standard colour.
- Premium colour.
- Black & white.
- White pages.
- Cream pages.
- A range of trim sizes and custom trim sizes.

For an on-demand printing service the options are great. However, the options you choose will have an impact on pricing and how much royalty you will be able to earn.

If your planner or journal has a colour interior, even if it's just one page Amazon will calculate the price for your whole design in colour. If you would like a colour interior then don't choose a hardcover, please choose a paperback. Hardcover with colour interiors massively increases the print price and shrinks your royalty. If you have designed your interior in black and white and have your cover either in black and white or in colour, then a hardcover can be a great option for you. In this case think about both a hardcover listing and a paperback listing, so your customers can choose depending on their budget and preference. Don't underestimate a clean monochrome design, it can look beautifully clean, professional and chic!

If you have a colour interior, then paperback is the way for you to go. This will allow you to maximise your royalty rather than shrink it. Paperback is the most profitable choice to make regardless of your design. You get to choose standard or premium colour and paper. There isn't a lot of difference when it comes to quality between standard and premium for the cost. Standard paper still provides a great outcome, but if you can afford to it may be worth considering premium. It will eat into your royalty but play about with the options to get the best outcome for you.

Glossy and matte covers is another option to choose between. It depends on your preference on how you would like your planner or journal to look and the finish you want to have. My clients do often ask for my advice on which is best, and I would always recommend glossy. This is because the cover has another layer on it to make it glossy. This makes it slightly more durable, it doesn't mark as easily as matte, your customer will use this every day so your planner and journal will get worn. If you're unsure you can order a proof in each finish so you can choose. These options don't affect your royalties. Amazon includes these costs in the printing outlay, both glossy and matte options have the same costs.

There are specific trim sizes you will have to stick to if you are choosing the hardcover option. If you are choosing paperback, there is a big selection of standard trim sizes to choose from, or you can opt for your own custom size. The trim size is your final size of your planner or journal. If you are a visual person you may have to draw the size out to visualise what size it will be. I know I do! Make your life easy, don't pick an obscure size. If you want to publish in both hardback and paperback have a look at which sizes are available in both.

THE PUBLISHING PROCESS

Self-publishing can seem a daunting and tricky process. Once you understand the basics, you will find your way. Here are some tips so you are less likely to get your listing rejected the first time you put your work up for review. This will help you save time and cause you less stress. The main thing is to ensure your measurements are correct for your manuscript and your cover. This can be one of the most frustrating things to get right if you are new to the process. Even if you are 1mm out on your cover or manuscript, your submission won't be approved. If errors are missed in the review, your planner or journal could be printed wrong, sometimes small errors can escape the Amazon KDP check and review system. There could be white lines printed around your work or text cut off, this is why you need to double-check your margin, trim and bleed measurements. Titling your planner or journal on Amazon KDP needs to be correct when making your KDP listing. I know this sounds obvious, but this can be one reason why Amazon can reject your submission. Ensure there is nothing offensive in your content and that you have the copyright to everything you are publishing, especially if you have used stock images. If you are using quotes in your design, please reference them. Keep to the Amazon KDP guidelines, if you need to read them, please visit the KDP website.

Writing a description of your planner or journal is important. You can have up to 4000 characters to write an amazing description about you and your planner or journal, but you can't upload any photos. When you see other planners and journals selling on Amazon, they are a physical product, they haven't been produced by Amazon KDP. Selling a physical product on Amazon allows you to upload your own photos and add your company or product branding to the listing. When you are listing a KDP book you have to rely on your cover and a cleverly put-together description, if you manufacture your planner or journal, you could list it on Amazon as a product. So, what should you write in your description? Yes, your customers will want to know the specifications of the planner but start with the transformation buying your publication will offer them, tell your story and why you have put your creation together. If you have ordered proofs of your planner or journal, then give these out to people to use in return for a review or feedback. This way you can also use their feedback in the write-up of your description.

Keywords are really important, do not leave this section blank. I have a great tip for you when it comes to looking for keywords. Go on to Amazon's main selling page and type in what your customers would to find your product, for example, food journal. There will be related searches come up underneath. These are all the keywords and phrases that people are using to search for that product. Use any of these in the keywords section on KDP. It will help your publication appear when these keywords are searched for. It's a great way to get your product in front of people who are searching for those exact words.

Categories are also important; these are how Amazon adds your publication to specific categories depending on what your publication is about. Please choose relevant categories. If your publication sells a certain number of copies in a short window it's more than likely to gain the number one or best seller status. Please don't focus on the number one position. Remember you are on a bigger journey than that and getting your planner or journal to the right people is more important. If the number one best-seller tag is important to you, do the work to build your audience and set up a marketing strategy for your launch.

You are publishing a low content book, this is how Amazon classes all planner's or journals. This means you don't have to purchase an ISBN number to publish your creation. If you choose to you will need to purchase this separately.

Once you have setup your listing it's time to upload your manuscript and cover. Now you will see if you have designed to the correct margins and if Amazon's automatic review check has picked up any errors. The great thing about KDP is that it has the launch viewer. Once you have uploaded your cover and manuscript files click on the launch viewer. This will allow you to see any errors with margins or with your design work. KDP will flag up any pages it detects an error on. This will show in the left panel of the launch viewer. It will also let you know if the cover size is unexpected for the size of the manuscript. It's not fool proof and there still can be errors, do a manual check too but the launch viewer is a great contingency to have.

When you are happy with your design, no errors are appearing on the launch viewer, and you have checked each page manually. You can approve your manuscript and cover file and set your price. The price is your choice. Amazon will let you know how much royalty you will make off each copy sold in the end right column and the minimum price that you can set. At the top of this page, you can choose which countries to sell your publication in. You can opt to sell worldwide or select individual countries. Again this is personal preference some people feel daunted at the thought of their publication going on sale around the world, it also depends on where you want to position your business and where your audience is based, your business may already be global. Or you may want to attract a more global audience.

I would recommend ordering a proof at this stage for yourself, before you submit your files for review. You need to see what your design looks like before anyone else buys it. This gives you time to amend your files if needed and really scrutinise what your design looks like when published on paper before your planner or journal listing goes live. You may love it, or you may decide it needs some tweaks and changes. Once you have received your proof, you've checked your design and you are happy with everything, you can submit your listing to Amazon for review. The reviewing process can take up to 72 business hours, but it can also take a little longer if they are busy. Please leave enough time for this process, if you are aiming for a specific launch date upload your manuscript for approval two weeks before. If you need to make any amendments and reupload you have time. You will receive an email when Amazon have approved your planner or journal. If they reject it don't worry. They will send you an email with the corrections you need to make. Make the corrections and reupload your corrected files and resubmit for approval. Please be aware that if you keep getting your files rejected and you are not fixing the problem, Amazon can block your account. I don't say this to scare you and if you are genuinely trying to fix the issue and Amazon reject your file again, please contact them, they will help you. Sometimes they are a little confusing on how they write emails making it hard to understand what the problem is. They can be quite technical.

Once your planner or journal has been published and your listing is live, you can order author copies. Customers and clients can also order their copies. Share your link far and wide, driving traffic to your Amazon publication is how you are going to get your sales! Don't leave this thinking because your publication is on Amazon you will sell thousands overnight - it very rarely if ever works like that. You need a strategy to allow you to get as many people seeing your planner or journal as possible. The next chapter will cover the launching process. This is where you see your very own planner or journal design come to life.

Key points to remember from this section-

- Decide between publishing or printing.
- Choose your specifications on Amazon KDP.
- Ensure your Amazon KDP listing is accurate.
- Order your proof.
- Submit your listing to Amazon KDP for approval.

Chapter
Five

GETTING YOUR PLANNER OR JOURNAL OUT
THERE

*a*t this stage, a lot of people hit the brakes and come to a grinding halt. Some of it is fear of not knowing what to do or fear of judgement. I've seen this happen many times and it is a daunting process. The idea that this amazing, beautiful creation is going into the world after all of these months of hard work is sometimes too much. I understand our minds can play tricks on us and fear can set in and paralyse us. We are all human. I want you to know that on the other side of putting your planner or journal out into the world you are going to help so many people. You are going to create an impact and you are going to grow your business. You need to grow your confidence, so this doesn't become a project that you leave and don't complete. Please don't let it be one of those projects! Your design will be far too good for that. Like the rest of this process let's break it down and make it a simpler process. Over-complicating any part isn't worth it. You know who your target audience is, so you know who you need to put your planner or journal in front of. You will know where to find them on the internet or off the internet. It's always a great idea to write your plan down of how you are going to get your creation out into the world. Think about timings, you don't want everything to be last minute and it's always good to create a build-up on interest before you launch. After all it's taken a lot of work to put together your planner or journal, you don't want to rush launching it.

Prepping this alongside your design project would be a good move. You can keep a list of ideas of where and how you can get your planner or journal out there and keep updating your launch plan as your ideas change or, you come up with new plans. How are you going to get your planner or journal in front of your ideal people? Have you thought about the following-

- Blogging.
- Guest blogging.
- Appearing on podcasts.
- Social media reels, stories, lives and posts.
- Magazines and Newspapers.
- Building & contacting your email list.
- Events.

These are just some suggestions, you don't have to choose, you can do them all or you can choose what feels right for you. Some might not be relevant, or you might have your own plan and ideas, that's great.

Having some time before you launch your planner or journal will make the process feel more structured and less rushed. Not everyone does this and it can make all the difference, ideally you want people to buy as soon as you launch. If you structure your launch, then you can build excitement and buzz for people to buy. People are always curious, but they will also want to know what transformation your planner or journal will offer them. Remember you sell by creating an emotional connection with the correct people. Tell them how your planner or journal will help them. Will it change their life? What problem solving does it offer to them?

Another way could be to create giveaways or offer an introductory price. This allows your customers and clients to bag your planner or journal at a great price and for you to sell more copies in a short amount of time. This could help you get to the number one spot but also rank top in the searches people are making. This means you get more eyes on your product and more purchases. Ultimately you are a business, and you want to sell, but don't come across salesy. Always think about everything you put out there from your customer's perspective and how you can help them, not how they can help you.

Below are the simple steps to launching your planner or journal:

- Preparation
- The Build Up
- The Offer
- Communicating Your Offer Everywhere

The key is to get as many eyes on your product as possible, so you may have to keep working on that because it can take time. Whether you are posting on social media groups or organically building your email list, everything is always growing if you are making it happen. If you do nothing your planner and journal will do nothing, you have to actively promote it.

 "Dreams become reality one choice at a time."

— UNKNOWN

TESTIMONIALS & FEEDBACK

Being able to gain social proof that your product is amazing and helps people transform their lives is exactly what you need. When you buy from a business that you may never have heard of before what is the first thing you do? Look for reviews and this could make or break the sale. Being able to offer future customers the reassurance that your product is everything they need, will pay so many dividends to your business in the future and it allows you to grow a bigger customer base. This may take time but small steps forward turns into something greater.

Amazon like to see your product receive 5-star reviews, it will allow your planner or journal to be shown to more people. People trust past customers' non-biased opinions, and this can turn them into a customer themselves and in turn, allow them to discover your business. Nothing is ever wasted, even if you get the shortest review in the world but it's positive, it will still add authenticity to your business and improve the trust of your product.

Your customers will need prompting to leave a review and you will need to think how you are going to do this. You can use a page at the front of your planner to thank your customer for their purchase. This gives you the opportunity to add a QR code to link your Amazon listing and ask for a review. You could offer an incentive, is there something you could send them once they've left you a review? This could be something digital like a download, you don't have to offer anything physical. Think about the logistics of this and maybe the system you would need to set up to offer this.

Unfortunately, people don't always leave a review, they forget because they are busy with life, so you need a prompt or incentivise them.

UPSELLING OTHER PRODUCTS OR SERVICES

Previously in this book I talked about the customer journey and that it isn't all about the royalties. The royalties are great, they are a lovely passive and semi-passive way to make an income and it's nice to see them drop into your bank account. The way you are going to make a return on your investment quicker is if you have a larger product or a service to upsell on the back of your planner or journal. If you have your marketing correct, you will be selling to your ideal customers already. They will be interested in what other offerings you have. If you sell 30 planners or journals in a month and 2 customers decide to take your course priced at £1995 then you have seen a return on your investment and made a profit.

Do you have a course, membership or a one to one service you can offer? These are perfect for making people aware of what they could sign up for. Dedicate a specific page in your planner or journal to tell them about your business and what you offer, tell your story about who you are, connect with your customer. Don't leave out the details of where they could sign up for your amazing offering. Always include a link, people want to make purchases easily, they will give up if you make it difficult for them, you could also include a QR code. They can scan it and be taken to the sales page for either your product or service. Include the handles to your social media, some may need more nurturing until they feel they are ready to make a bigger purchase, where can they make more of a connection with you? Social media business pages and Facebook groups are a great place for this.

MAKING FUTURE CHANGES

Once you have designed and launched your planner or journal it doesn't always mean the journey is over. If you have designed your publication yourself, you will be able to go back and amend anything after receiving feedback. If you have used Amazon publishing, you will also be able to make your edits straight away. If you have used a printing service, you will have to commission another print run. Publishing with Amazon KDP in the first instance may be beneficial for you to receive feedback before letting a printer's print hundreds of copies. I don't want anything to hold you back to develop your idea further or to make a series of planners and journals to help others. Maybe future editions in different areas of life or teaching different things. Always think bigger and push the boundaries of possibility. If you have found this process hard, don't let that put you off going through it again because it will be easier next time. The more you go through the process the more refined your designs will become and the publishing process will become just another method you know. Like I said at the start any creative process is never linear, it circles back on itself several times, mainly because it becomes developmental, ideas change, or the project takes amazing twists and turns, and a beautiful journey unfolds before you. Make sure you always go on that journey in the future when planning new projects or tweaking the old.

Key points to remember from this section-

- Overcome any fear you may have about releasing your planner or journal into the world.
- Plan how you are going to launch and where you are going to advertise your planner or journal.
- Structure your launch.
- Gain testimonials or reviews on Amazon or your other platforms.
- Think about future projects.

THE END OF OUR JOURNEY TOGETHER

I hope you have enjoyed being curious and understanding the process of what it takes to put together a planner or a journal. I hope it has also given you different things to think about and made you see planner and journal design differently. There are so many ways of getting your creation out into the world, it doesn't have to be a rigid process. If something isn't working for you, remember to find a way around it, problem solve but don't give up on your dream.

I hope this book has broken down the barriers and made everything seem easier so you can develop and create the very best product by the end. Be excited for what is to come and be inspired to create something amazing. Be reassured you can create your dreams even if you might have to compromise with certain things in the first instance. Everything is a work in progress and where you start is not where you will end up. I hope this has given you a starting point and a process to follow so you can work your magic on your own planner or journal. Enjoy working on it on a deeper level with a deeper understanding, so you know you will produce something really valuable. This will allow you to stand out and show your expertise in your field, gain recognition and a reputation with your knowledge and grow your business.

Your project is complete!

Congratulations, it's time to celebrate!

What's Next

If you are still daunted by the process or you feel you haven't got time to take this on yourself, please reach out for support. At The Printable Life ™ I offer one to one design packages. This is a "done for you" bespoke service. We can get your dream planner or journal uniquely designed for your business and published within around 12 weeks. There are no templates used, just beautiful bespoke branded designs to set you apart from everyone else. Remember there is always a solution to every problem and asking for help is fine. Never be afraid to invest in yourself and your business, you will be adding an amazing asset that will pay dividends to you in years to come.

Here is the QR link below for our design packages-

1-1 Design Packages Link

www.theprintablelife.enlitly.com/site/designpackagesall

The support my clients receive is amazing. If you still want to design your planner or journal, then this is fabulous! As you can see through this book, I will always encourage people to find their own creativity. Maybe you feel you need a little extra guidance alongside this book? I have put together a course where you can learn in your own time and have life-time access. I guide you through all the steps, planning, designing and publishing, and how this is all possible using Canva. On the course you have access to the process, resources and my knowledge so you can create your own planner or journal vision. Not only that, but you also have access to it forever so you can create multiple versions.

Here is the QR link for the course-

The Course Link

www.theprintablelife.enlitly.com/product/plandesignpublish

You have a great journey ahead, I'm so excited for you. There are so many options and I know you will achieve your planner or journal dream.

I would also love to know what you create whether that is through the information in this book or if you have enrolled yourself on my course, I would love to hear from you. Drop me a message on my social media to let me know.

Enjoy the process and love your journey, everyone's journey is different. Move forward to design your planner and journal vision for your business, create an impact in your business and to the people's lives who you're designing for.

Above all, remember-

> "Our goals can only be reached through a vehicle of a plan, in which we must fervently believe, and upon which we must vigorously act. There is no other route to success."

— STEPHEN A. BRENNAN

Love

Michelle
x

Kind
Words

"Michelle was brilliant all the way through the process. Nothing was too much trouble, Michelle answered all my questions and offered great advice along the way. And the outcome was a perfect planner that I love."

— GILL MOORE, FATIGUED TO FABULOUS

"Omgggggg!!!! I freakin love Michelle and I really love the planner and journal she helped me bring to life. She did an awesome job. She is very professional and a pleasure to work with. I definitely recommend her services!!!!!"

— ONATAH ISIS EL, FEMININE FLOW
AWARENESS

"Today, I'd like to thank someone who, if it wasn't for their help and commitment, I wouldn't have managed to achieve my dream of becoming a published author.

Last Christmas, I had a dream to create a Marketing Planner, to help entrepreneurs get more marketing done on their businesses. However, I had no clue about how to turn that dream into a reality.

Michelle's hard work turned my ideas, scribbled layouts and typed-up words into the ENTRE-PRENEURS MARKETING, SOCIAL MEDIA & BUSINESS PLANNER! She also helped me create the accompanying TO-DO Log and note-book with her amazing design skills too!

So, huge thanks, Michelle, for helping me achieve my dream. And for helping me to find an additional way to help busy freelancers, solo entrepreneurs and small business owners make marketing their businesses more manageable. It still makes me smile that I can put my name into Amazon and my books come up!"

— COLETTE BRATTON, SMALL BUSINESS EQUALISER

"Michelle was an absolute pleasure from beginning to end. She was always available for any questions/concerns. She was able to bring my thoughts and dreams to reality. She was there every step of the way to guide and help and now I can say my journal is officially published!!!! She was a godsend you will not be disappointed!!"

— BRITTANY BATTISE, HEART & SOUL LLC

"I absolutely love working with Michelle - she really is passionate about putting your project together as if it is her project too. The attention to detail and the amount of work that goes into working with Michelle was an absolute dream. She really cares about bringing your vision to life and will really go the extra mile to make sure that happens.

Thank you for making my vision a reality 🖤 appreciate you so much - I have in the past recommended my clients to Michelle and will definitely continue to do so."

— TABASSUM SABIR, BE.YOU.TIFUL –
EMOTIONAL MASTERY COACHING

Working with Michelle on the design and publication of My Pink Planner was such a positive and uplifting experience.

At first, I was unsure how Michelle would interpreted all of the information I had been collating through my breast cancer journey. Would she be able to create my vision? Would she be able to encompass everything I wanted tracking on one page? Would the design be in the style I was wanting to portray to others going through the ups and downs of a cancer diagnosis and treatment?

All of my worries were squashed as soon as the first draft came through. Michelle's adaptability and understanding of my needs were spot on. After a couple of design sessions Michelle also created the aesthetics of the planner just how I envisaged them.

The whole experience, from start to finish was exceptional and now I have a planner to help others with an unfortunate cancer diagnosis, plan and organise their treatment journey.

— KELLY WILKINSON, MY PINK PLANNER

About The Author

The Printable Life ™ was born out of a lightbulb moment in 2020. In the midst of a pandemic Michelle Chitty decided to put her creativity to good use and help others. She started designing and selling printables to help people be organised in life and business.

Michelle wanted to help others create something that would have more impact on the world. With Michelle's decade of design experience along with her love and skill of being a born organiser, planner and journal packages were carefully put together. Offering publishing instead of printing allowed a more affordable approach so all business owners and entre-preneurs no matter their stage of business, could invest in a bespoke branded planner or journal.

Michelle started to realise that adding a planner or journal to a business was so much more than about money. As well as creating an extra income stream for businesses, there were multiple benefits including the positioning of a business owner's expertise.

The beautifully bespoke designed planners and journals by The Printable Life ™ made way for other opportunities for clients that had worked with Michelle. From starting brand new businesses to invitations on to podcasts and running workshops. The addition of a Printable Life ™ planner or journal opened new doors and opportunities for business growth for Michelle's clients.

Michelle is a creative entrepreneur working in the surroundings of the West Yorkshire countryside. She loves to walk for miles and gets inspired on the way, it's where her best ideas are thought about!

You can learn more about Michelle and The Printable Life™ by connecting on social media, scan the QR codes below:

Instagram

Facebook

Pinterest

instagram.com/theprintablelife

facebook.com/theprintablelife

pinterest.com/theprintablelifeuk

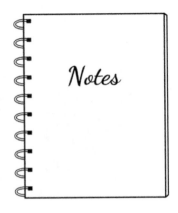

Give yourself permission to scribble, make notes and enjoy the creative process!

Notes

♥

♥

♥

♥

♥

♥

♥

♥

♥

♥

♥

♥

♥

♥

♥

♥

♥

♥

♥

♥

♥

♥

♥

♥

♥

♥

♥

♥

♥

♥

♥

♥

♥

♥

♥

♥

♥

♥

♥

♥

♥

♥

♥

♥

♥

♥

♥

♥

♥

♥

♥

♥

♥

♥

♥

♥

♥

♥

♥

♥

♥

♥

♥

♥

♥

♥

♥

♥

♥

♥

♥

♥

♥

♥

♥

♥

♥

♥

♥

♥

♥

♥

♥

♥

♥

♥

♥

♥

♥

♥

♥

♥

♥

♥

♥

♥

♥

♥

♥

♥

♥

♥

♥

♥

♥

♥

♥

♥

♥

♥

♥

♥

♥

♥

♥

♥

♥

♥

♥

♥

♥

♥

♥

♥

♥

♥

♥

♥

♥

♥

♥

♥

♥

♥

♥

♥

♥

♥

♥

♥

♥

♥

♥

♥

♥

♥

♥

♥

♥

♥

♥

♥

♥

♥

♥

♥

♥

♥

♥

♥

♥

♥

♥

♥

♥

♥

♥

♥

♥

♥

♥

♥

♥

♥

♥

♥

♥

♥

♥

♥

♥

♥

♥

♥

♥

♥

♥

♥

♥

♥

♥

♥

♥

♥

♥

♥

♥

♥

♥

♥

♥

♥

♥

♥

♥

♥

♥

♥

♥

♥

♥

♥

♥

♥

♥

♥

♥

♥

♥

♥

♥

♥

♥

♥

♥

♥

♥

♥

♥

♥

♥

♥

♥

♥

♥

♥

♥

♥

♥

♥

♥

♥

♥

♥

♥

♥

♥

♥

♥

♥

♥

♥

♥

♥

♥

♥

♥

♥

♥

♥

♥

♥

♥

♥

♥

♥

♥

♥

♥

♥

♥

♥

♥

♥

♥

♥

♥

♥

♥

♥

♥

♥

♥

♥

♥

♥

♥

♥

♥

♥

♥

♥

♥

♥

♥

♥

♥

♥

♥

♥

♥

♥

♥

♥

♥

♥

♥

♥

♥

♥

♥

♥

♥

♥

♥

♥

♥

♥

♥

♥

♥

♥

♥

♥

♥

♥

♥

♥

♥

♥

♥

♥

- ♥
- ♥
- ♥
- ♥
- ♥
- ♥
- ♥
- ♥
- ♥
- ♥
- ♥
- ♥
- ♥
- ♥
- ♥
- ♥
- ♥

♥

♥

♥

♥

♥

♥

♥

♥

♥

♥

♥

♥

♥

♥

♥

♥

♥

♥

♥

♥

♥

♥

♥

♥

♥

♥

♥

♥

♥

♥

♥

♥

♥

♥

Printed in Great Britain
by Amazon

25285164R00076